Anam Chara
Oracle

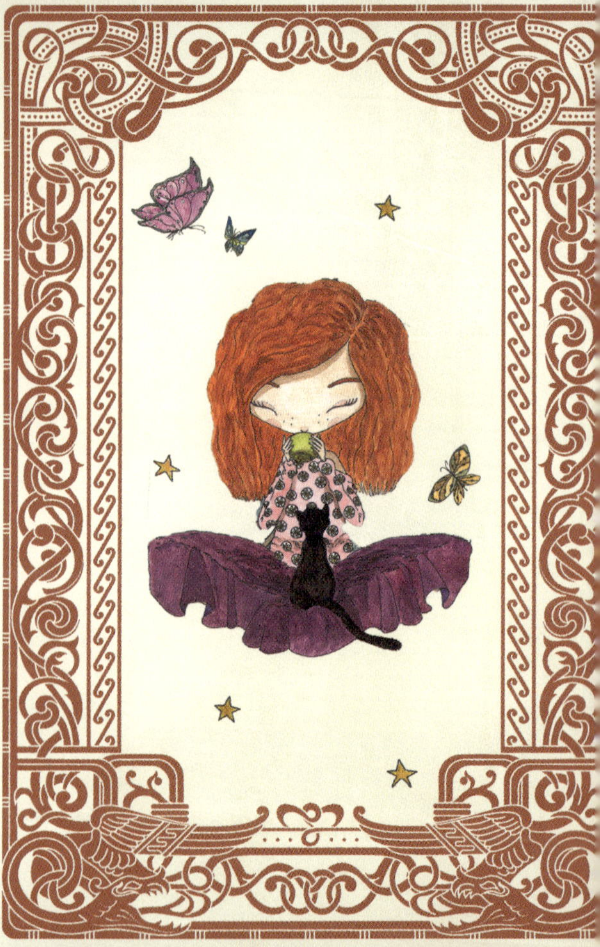

Anam Chara

ORACLE

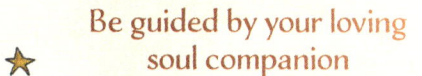

Be guided by your loving
soul companion

SAORSA SIONNACH

ROCKPOOL

A Rockpool book
PO Box 252
Summer Hill
NSW 2130
Australia

rockpoolpublishing.com
Follow us! f 🅾 rockpoolpublishing
Tag your images with #rockpoolpublishing

ISBN: 9781922786029

Published in 2024 by Rockpool Publishing
Copyright text and illustrations © Saorsa Sionnach 2024
Copyright design © Rockpool Publishing 2024

All rights reserved. No part of this publication may be reproduced, stored in a retrieval system, or transmitted in any form or by any means, electronic, mechanical, photocopying, recording or otherwise, without the prior written permission of the publisher.

Design and typesetting by Alissa Dinallo, Rockpool Publishing
Edited by Lisa Macken

Printed and bound in China
10 9 8 7 6 5 4 3 2 1

SPARKS

This work is for Mana, the golden lion, and Gabriel, my lighthouse in all storms. I thank you for your gentle touch and unshakable patience. Your wisdom is my sparkling river running in the forest.

For supporting me each day and loving me in all my quirkiness I will be endlessly grateful to you, my darling husband. Loving you back to the moon and beyond, until we are stardust . . .

And to Angeline, my favourite hearth witch and the best sister I could have wished for, you are a true blessing.

CONTENTS

Introduction: nesting	1
How to use the cards: map	6
Card spreads: stardust	7
Anamchara Oracle cards	13
1. Life flame	14
2. Unity	16
3. Creative thinking	18
4. Vessel	20
5. Alchemist	22
6. Admiration	24
7. Sharing	26
8. Trust	28
9. Elders	30
10. Scars	32
11. Seer	34
12. Secret garden	36
13. Sequence	38
14. Crone	40
15. Seed	42
16. Enlightenment	44
17. Initiation	46
18. Depths	48
19. Star	50
20. Taking off	52

21. Balance ... 54
22. Knight ... 56
23. Wounds ... 58
24. Mountain ... 60
25. Hermit ... 62
26. Fate ... 64
27. Thief ... 66
28. Crossroads ... 68
29. Masterpiece ... 70
30. Home ... 72
31. Construction ... 74
32. Pilgrim ... 76
33. Witch ... 78
34. Fire ... 80
35. Water ... 82
36. Air ... 84
37. Earth ... 86
38. Shadow ... 88
39. Light ... 90
40. Midnight sun ... 92
41. Yule ... 94
42. Ostara ... 96
43. Litha ... 98
44. Mabon ... 100

About the author and illustrator ... 103

INTRODUCTION: NESTING

Each one of us has their own way of translating their perceptions into emotions, knowledge and skills. This is the very definition of our unique being: how what we look at through the spying glass is transformed. We are shapers of reality, which is why I would never tell you your reality is wrong. We just share concepts and images that help us understand each other and cross the bridge between our realities. Of course, society, education and reference frames shape us as well, but our singularity resides in our very differences and similarities beyond any cultural implication. This is why love is a universal language and art needs no words.

In the rushed world we live in it is tricky to comprehend the difference between our own movement, divine movement and the restless turbulence of our minds. Silence brings balance, truth and peace, so it is in stillness we find the wave of the universe and forget about meaningless agitation.

Nothing should define you if it hasn't come from within. You are the only one to take on this journey and the only one able to reach the point of consciousness. No one else can see your truth or understand you as yourself, so take that path with compassion and be sensitive to your feelings along the way. You are not alone: individuality doesn't mean loneliness. As we thrive as one, we complete each other. We do not imagine the world deprived of one of its elements, do we? We are a wonderful and immeasurable web of talents, sensibilities and perceptions, which if moved in harmony become one reality.

In the Celtic culture an anamchara is a soul friend, invisible confidant or spirit adviser. Even centuries ago it was commonly accepted that these friends were among us. Some say they are an invisible part of you, and it is true as we are all one, but let's not strip them from their personality. As the fox, the owl, the wind, the snow and you or me, they are. They are eternal light sitting in the present moment and seeing beauty in imperfection and perfection. This flicker is within us as well, and we are all very capable of connecting with those friends. We just need the right conjunction and to welcome it, then as signs they will spread all through our daily lives.

Close your eyes; the reign of darkness is nothing more than peace. In its silence beats the soul of the source. It is your essence. You are strength, this whole, wandering shadow and pulsing light. You are the sun, the stars and the matter that composes them. You are the everything and the nothing, movement and stillness, the life that blooms and the death that caresses it like a mother cares for her child. Imagine floating among that wonder, changing its very shape – this is your divine nature. The anamchara, the friendly spirit who walks by your side, is the guardian of its memory, here to open your eyes to the past, present and future, to wholeness. Be grateful, for you always have a companion watching over you without judgement.

You were once an anamchara, at the beginning of all. We are brothers and sisters of the universe, souls like stars dancing in the waves of beauty, and as a breath drawn like the wind in a grass field we chose life: to know what it was to feel, in the body as much as in the soul, to fly, be a bird, give birth, swim like dolphins, share physical love and sense the flames of the sun licking our scales, skin or feathers. We chose, despite all fears . . . and we forgot, in the process of embodiment. We were born, we died, and we were born again.

There started the long apprenticeship of who we are and our completeness. Life after life, lesson after lesson, births after deaths, through all bodies and shapes we touched our soul and the divine source that makes us one. With the greatest patience, the Anamchara instils hope and love to guide us toward our home.

The memory loss we suffered detached us from our true nature, igniting in us the burning desire to reconnect. That feeling of missing something crucial disappears once everything comes into place and we acknowledge our nature. You don't need to remember past lives, seek the absolute truth or tame any demon within to be complete. Just listen to your heart, because the anamchara is whispering to you there. Know that the anamchairde will never feel wrong or judgemental. They are the very definition of hope, as they thrive in pushing us to become our best selves.

These guardian spirits can be met in many cultures under many names, sometimes as sylphs or wind itself. They are messengers of the divine. Brigid of Kildare said about them in the Martyrology of Óengus: 'Anyone without a soul friend is like a body without a head.' However, do not think they are only our conscience, as they are much more than this: they are our spiritual builders.

In this life, as in all of them, we seek our truth through spiritual growth, but nothing is fixed. Our journey isn't all lined up. We have chosen for ourselves to intuitively learn how to get back to our true selves through a path we still have the freedom to go against, even when it is painful. We are not dragged toward destiny. We are the ones who shape our storylines, and whether it is full of drama or a peaceful path is our doing. Consciously or unconsciously we are writing our solas leabhar or 'book of light', the tale of how we became and are becoming.

This oracle is an expression of the connection between us and our anamchara friends. It will guide you and allow you to make your own way to the anamchairde, to navigate through light and shadow, doubt and certainties to seize your truth and peace and establish your connection with this hope that lies within you and within everyone. Enjoy the journey. May you discover your north, wee dragonflies.

So mote it be.

HOW TO USE THE CARDS: MAP

Each card in this oracle is a channelled message from an anamchara and has a hand-painted illustration that was realised intuitively, a title followed by keywords and an incantation, a short text to explain the meaning of the card and an action you might like to undertake. You can use the deck in many ways to bring you clues and keys on how to take action on your question. You may prefer to use elements you see in the drawings for your interpretation or refer to the text in this booklet but you also have the incantations, which are like short poems that were worked so their energy flows to enhance your intention and help keep your mind on your goals. Feel free to use them in any way that feels right for you.

The incantations are not just for magic practitioners. You may be new to witchcraft or have no interest in it whatsoever, but this does not mean this text is useless: you can use the incantations as mantras, focusing your intention on the progress you seek from the card you have drawn. For those doing magic, the incantations can be used in a ritual to work on your aim and make it sharper or increase the magic of your spell. It may take place on your altar as a focal point or energy to highlight until you've worked out your issue.

CARD SPREADS: STARDUST

The card spreads below may help you get comfortable with readings. If you want to use only the guidance or the image or create your own feeling behind the name of each card, feel free to do so.

Anamchara spread

For a clear question that is brief and well defined draw just one card, which will be enough to bring some element of answer just as a rune or tarot card would. It is not always in quantity that a message is better given. This is also great as a daily pull.

Triptych spread

This spread, in which you draw three cards that represent the mind, body and soul, will give you a complete view of where you stand on different levels.

Elements spread

For this spread draw four cards, which represent:

- **Card 1,** water, human level: your emotional state.

- **Card 2,** air, divine connection: elaborate thinking, what you shape.

- **Card 3,** earth, human level: the material aspects of your life, family, work and so on.

- **Card 4,** fire, divine connection: spirituality vs ego.

Seasons spread

The season cards can be used for time prediction or energy readings, and also for their symbols similar to the other cards. Note that the festival times are relevant to the northern hemisphere but they can be adapted in both hemispheres. For this spread draw four cards, which represent:

- **Card 1,** spring/Ostara: the lesson to be learned.

- **Card 2,** summer/Litha: the talents you can rely on.

- **Card 3,** autumn/Mabon: what is obsolete.

- **Card 4,** winter/Yule: the inspiration that is needed.

Angel wings spread

For this spread draw seven cards, which represent:

- ♥ **Card 1:** the heart of the topic.
- ♥ **Card 2:** the present.
- ♥ **Card 3:** the past.
- ♥ **Card 4:** your fears.
- ♥ **Card 5:** external influences.
- ♥ **Card 6:** the next step.
- ♥ **Card 7:** the outcome.

The art of cartomancy or fortune telling is based on your habit of handling cards and also on your appropriation. By 'appropriation' I don't mean taking a cultural belief or practice and arranging it to your own taste, which may lead to disaster, but adapting what you understand from reference frames you come across and building your own religion that is true to what speaks to you with respect and love. Your individuality is shaped by your life experiences, the music you listen to, the movies you react to and the books that stay with you forever. You adapt what you understand from them to design an intuitive practice that respects your beliefs.

Keep a journal so you can review your spreads to see how far you have progressed. What lessons have been repeated? What obstacles did you manage to overcome? Your journal will be an endless resource on your learning path.

ANAM CHARA ORACLE CARDS

1. LIFE FLAME

Self-love, divine self

Spark that brings all matter to life, I am divine and I am human; in both I bloom

All things passing on this earth carry in them the primal flame, the thrust of life. In this spark nests your soul, and also the whole beauty of your choice to become incarnate. You are, already, even unfinished. You are in the grace of perfection and the laugh of imperfection. Your thoughts are awakening and your life awaits the grandiose unfolding of your adventure.

∞ 11 ∞

Respect this flame and nurture it with joy and hope, because if life is a blank canvas your perception of reality will feed your fire or stifle it by fear.

Your free will is the essential tool for your growth. By coming to live on earth you have chosen to know humanity's strengths and weaknesses in order to be complete. Do not be a judge: be a pilgrim. Marvel at all things, including yourself. The anamchairde will lead you if you become aware of them.

※

Action: meditate. Sit in a comfy position and put on quiet music that makes you feel safe. Anchor yourself to tune in to the universe, feeling the energy of source within and around you. Dare to say this mantra: 'I am a divine being,' and allow the visions to come to you. Your anamchara is eager to meet with you, so let them guide you through your inner journey. Don't doubt yourself and don't judge your experience, because it is yours to make.

2. UNITY

Interconnection, mirror effect

Through the veil of all that lives and dies,
I see the pieces of the same light

If you take the time to focus on your inner flicker of light you will quickly realise it doesn't shine on its own. This light connects you with others and, better yet, teaches you that we are all of the same essence. Humans, animals, plants – all living beings – incarnate as a unique higher being. We are in our purest state of love.

Your anamchara invites you to have a look at the world around you and try to feel this connection. It is not always easy, obviously, but if you acknowledge the frames that have been erected you will experience the bond between us all. Because we are one, what you do will inspire others and what you share will be shared again. When we are filled with fear we become aggressive and critical, but when we are filled with confidence we free ourselves from limitations. Together we create tomorrow's world. Never forget that the universe constantly shows you mirrors so you get the opportunity to improve.

Action: understand you are never alone. With new eyes, consider others as part of you with their fears, hopes and questions. Try to look at the situation without judgement. When you have a disagreement with someone, instead of instinctively defending your position put yourself in their skin. It is not easy, but you'll soon realise their reaction comes from fear or misunderstanding, just as you fear or misunderstand. Meet them halfway to reconcile.

3. CREATIVE THINKING

Visualisation, mental focus

On the edge of emptiness, spirit,
help this world to be shaped

Your awareness of yourself, the universe around you and the complex web that connects us all are what make you mindful of the universal reality. You are, as a being. René Descartes said 'I think therefore I am.' Our thoughts, as much as our actions, are what make us what we are and what we live and experience on a daily basis.

This thought is fuel for reality, for creation. Every thought sets in motion the adventure of tomorrow, and consciously or unconsciously your power resides there. Peter Pan used the fairy dust of happy thoughts to allow children to fly, and your very own story is built the same way. The existing limits to your potential are the only ones you force on yourself. Mark Twain wrote 'They did not know it was impossible, so they did it,' a sentence that embodies perfectly the power of creative thinking, of taking on its full dimension when you reflect on your potential. It is up to you how you work your magic, because it is very real and it occurs daily, in each passing moment.

Action: record your projects in detail to give them shape, not leaving anything out. Devote some time to what brings a smile to your face and let the feeling fuel you to go forth. Every day brings you a step closer, every time you smile that positive energy is deeper within you. Don't discard ideas because they seem unrealistic or messy; give them the space they need to exist. Show the world you have so much to offer.

Blessed be my body, as the vessel and its shepherd

4. VESSEL

Self-care, body respect

Blessed be my body, as the vessel
and its shepherd

One of the most difficult lessons for your eternal soul to understand is accepting the imperfection of your incarnation, especially when you are stuck in the fragility of a mortal body. However, your anamchara wants you to understand the sublime beauty settled within you. That body of yours is a temple, one you chose when you decided to experience life. Cherish it, respect it, admire it and take care of it. Never would you be as ungracious regarding a loved one's body than you are with your own, so why are you blaming this mortal coil, this vessel that is yours? Certainly it is small and narrow for the immortal vastness of your soul, but it was also a choice of yours with every one of its limitations. You once thought it was perfect as it was to welcome you.

Of course, no one is perfect, no one has a soul essence similar to yours: it carries your eternity, your unity to all other souls. However, your body has the extraordinary mission of making you experience humanity in ways impossible for your soul alone to do. Your body is the reason for your presence on earth, the manifestation of your choice. Be wise enough to treat it as such.

※

Action: pamper yourself and work on self-love. Any self-care works – it can be a bubble bath with essential oils and candles or a hike in nature – but make sure you reconnect with your body and make peace with it. It is not your enemy, but the closest friend you have. Every trigger is meant to warn you about something deeper and unconscious.
Treat it as a friend.

5. ALCHEMIST

Magic, intention, action

I am the artist of my power,
my magic becoming reality

You are going forth on your life path and awakening in divine achievement. It is time to recognise the tools given to you by your incarnation. Thoughts ignite creation, but they need to be embodied just like you are. In order to express your power in daily life and enhance your experience in the visible world, seize the tools at hand. Consider yourself an alchemist:

matter – the visible and invisible, anything that is thought – can be shaped and its transmutation is your art. You constantly modify reality, and if your thoughts create tomorrow's world you need to feel them. You are through all of your senses, so nurture them to embody your vision.

The spark of creation will gradually become reality when you give it form through images and emotions. Project yourself into a consciousness where this dream has become real and experience all the feelings that flow from it. It's no longer your mind that thinks but your body that gives it shape.

Action: make a vision board so you can look at your thoughts regularly, shaping them like a potter does with his vase and admiring it in such a way that you are bathing in the feeling of its realisation. Your vision board can be a collection of images that make you feel the way you'd be if it were done, a playlist or a series of craft projects. The more intention you throw into it the better. To make something sacred you need to devote your energy to it.

Spirit knows no time; the present is my eternity, as a gift

6. ADMIRATION

Meditation, attention to details

Spirit knows no time; the present
is my eternity, as a gift

It doesn't matter whether you perfectly know your daily environment, because the gift to marvel is offered by each and every experience and you can nurture it in your daily tasks.

Stop a moment, whisper the anamchairde. Have you ever realised how modern life is just a frantic race where, like a puppet, you painfully and laboriously learn to juggle work and your social and private lives? It is necessary to be contemplative in your existence in order to live things in depth. Take time to see through your experiences, to be at the heart of what you are doing rather than already running away to your next project or tasks such as picking up the children from school on time, doing the dinner shopping or studying for an exam.

Stop! The world belongs to its admirers. The smallest of tasks requires as much dedication as the most complex. Walk within yourself to discover the sensations of this body. You eat this bread, this seed, the wind and the rain, and become the earth. Everything becomes a miracle; everything is consciousness.

Action: exercise the art of contemplation. There are millions of ways to admire the tiny details of life: appreciate the work of those who made your clothes or seek the flow of the river when you turn on a tap. Your perception of reality highly influences your ability to be grateful and happy. If you are conscious enough of the movements of the universe within everything you start to understand your place in the big picture.

7. SHARING

Companionship, show yourself

I renounce my mask,
so I am seen by my kin

To participate in your reality it is necessary to express your truths. Because you are linked to and one with all other beings, you need to share the depth of your being. Whether it is a moment with a stranger or the discovery of new friends, if you search with your heart the universe will present you with soul companions.

Your inner self wants to express and share its points of view with others. Because connection with others can only be established with honesty and respect, expose your true nature so you can find soul mates who will understand you. This world is vast, and your soul family is waiting and wishing for you. Shine and they'll find you; open up and let people surprise you for the better. Your anamchara reminds you that as one, we can understand each other without the masks of social and cultural preconceptions. Love is universal.

Action: make some friends or spend time with yours. Seek alike spirits to enjoy some true moments of happiness and avoid people who belittle you or make you feel drained. It is important to stay true to yourself and connect with similar souls as this will nurture your growth. To do so, you need to dare show what you are. You are a unique piece of art, of love, even if you are a mess, and even your mess can bring you to your higher self. Just act out of respect for your true nature.

8. TRUST

Letting go, believing

I walk the thread that spirit weaved,
no matter how: if seen or in the dark

In order to experience something extraordinary a leap of faith is required, a risk taking. This moment now is for you, so forget your need to control things. You have set your creation in motion and shouldn't try to put yourself in the place of the universe. Let it work for you, as all the magic of your power resides here. Your intention gave birth to the movement of the universe, now let go. Trust that your anamchara is there for you.

You know the magic is happening, so don't try to figure it out or, worse, control it. Trust the universe: your power, your divinity and your creative essence. Cinderella didn't ask her good fairy godmother how her dress was made or why she had to be home by midnight. She welcomed the gift made to her without asking any questions, and you need to do the same. Be innocent and shout 'I believe in fairies,' and don't worry about understanding everything. It is sometimes confusing for your human understanding.

Action: because you are a creator but don't have a handle on all aspects of what you create or how you bring the universe to make it happen you sometimes need to just trust this force. Believe it is moving things for your best interest and welcome what is to come.

9. ELDERS

Akashic records, universal wisdom

Knowledge is a meadow, where
any flower is for me to pick

Your anamchara is trying to tell you that you have too little awareness of your real potential, so allow yourself the possibility of accessing the universal knowledge it holds. The knowledge is there and asks only to be used. This is not to do with intuition, but with a specific connection with the great encyclopaedia of universes. You can understand everything you touch provided your mind is ready to accept truths that do not correspond with your initial beliefs. It is a big step to take, but if you ask you shall receive.

Some people call this wisdom the Akashic records while others give it another name, but regardless of what it is called it relies on human concepts to accept the magnitude of what it represents. If you come to source with a wise mind the answers to your questions will be revealed to you in full light. For this, reflect, take time to listen rather than speak and above all to have an open heart.

Action: seek advice from someone older or with more experience and meditate to find your truth. Some answers can be found only from within but need an insight from your ancestors. You can touch these by reconnecting with the universal source with humility and the desire to grow. Light a candle and ask for access to ancient wisdom, leaving a feather as a sign of your willingness to learn.

10. SCARS

Old habits, transgenerational memories

The scars I carry for my ancestors,
I also heal for them

You have chosen to experience incarnated life and discover human feelings, even uneasy ones. By making this choice you have separated yourself from the original source, where universal knowledge and memory dwell. In order to learn from your embodied experience you need more than one lifetime to reveal the full extent of the iceberg that is your eternal soul.

It is not damaged over lifetimes; on the contrary, it is released as you learn from your life lessons.

You have hidden a lot of yourself: it lies beyond the shadow that came to you with the original fear born of physical pain and death and has distilled and spread like a virus. You carry the baggage of the fears that are passed on from your lifetimes and soul families, generation after generation and incarnation after incarnation. It is essential to cleanse yourself of these memories in order to change your behaviour and freely move forward. When pain is expressed, sometimes even physically, to lift the burden you must embrace the trial with appreciation. Otherwise you are Sisyphus, madly repeating rituals that have lost their meaning. Make room for your divine memory by shedding the painful memories of your past.

Action: do some shadow work on emotions that do not belong to you and journal your thoughts so you can grow out of those emotions. Look at yourself from outside so you can remain kind and objective. You will discern what does not belong to your fear and be able to get rid of it.

11. SEER

Intuition versus mind

If in the maze I trust the path,
I'll see clearly where spirit leads

If a decision comes that torments you there is clearly a disconnect between your mind and soul. Your mind too often calls on the way of reason and pushes you to make the 'right' choices, but are they based on what is fair: other people, social rank, worldly aspirations or a cultural and social framework that you desperately try to stick to?

Try allowing the way of your mind to express itself, because it seeks to protect you after all and means you no harm. Where it is totally wrong is that it wants to allow you to survive and thrive in an external context; however, this frame of reference doesn't correspond to you but rather to social norms you believe are part of you. The truth is that it does not serve you: quite the contrary. The only path to follow is that of your intuition, taking no heed of the risks, mistakes or missteps. This path is unique, perfectly suited to your being, and it will make you wiser and stronger.

Action: review all your options while facing a decision however small or big it is. Wonder why they are options: is it something you want? The answer should be as simple as the fact that it makes you happy or it does not. Although external factors enter into the equation you have control over your life through your own choice making. When you are pushed toward a path that makes you uncomfortable, seek within you the strength to see through the obligation.

12. SECRET GARDEN

Soul guide, divine connection, protection

Anamchara: whisper to my ear if I listen, and I will raise my hope when I despair

Your existence is a vast ball where everything revolves around you. Temptations and illusions are numerous and you often forget what you are behind the mundane and its shallow games. The way of your heart allows you to recognise the dissociation of your mind from the expression of your soul, and the garden teaches you to maintain this link between your conscience and inner voice.

Call your guides, spirit guardian or higher self and really listen to them. How do you differentiate them from the rest of the stream? It's simple: consciousness is pure love. Listening to this voice will make you feel confident without vulnerability because it radiates divine light. It doesn't matter whether you believe in a god or gods, because this light of love is undeniably within you and only asks to accompany you toward your happiness. Let it help you grow; let its power wash over you as you will never regret listening to it. Like an escape into an enchanted garden, cultivate moments to converse with your light.

Action: sit down and deeply breathe in and out. Get grounded. Visualise a garden where you feel safe, your inner haven, and once there ask your guardian to manifest themselves. They will always show up in a form that is non-threatening so you are not afraid. Keep trying until you get in touch and don't ever believe that you are not good enough to do it. Your guardians crave the opportunity to touch you on a conscious level.

13. SEQUENCE

Inception, evolution, trials

Bare as the truth, I pass the trial by fire to grow in spirit

You have the ability to be reborn like a phoenix. The little and big deaths you constantly experience will transform you and bring you closer or distance you from your divine being. When you draw Sequence you are on your way to transformation. If the prospect is terrifying because change bringing with it the unknown always frightens you, this is a significantly positive point. Your anamchara is showing you that you are ready: your experience has brought you to this culminating point, without return, where it is finally possible and necessary to change. If at first glance this change hurts you, do not fight it but rather embrace it, because the more you resist the more difficult it will be. If you are at this stage of your incarnation you are able to endure.

You choose the trials you will undertake on the long journey of the soul toward original memory and the full powers of your divine consciousness, and for those you must confront your mistakes and failures. Just like a toad or beast in fairy tales, let the prince express themselves and flourish.

Action: make a ritual to say goodbye to a part of you or a phase of your life that is no longer needed. Write a letter from the new-you point of view while sending love to the old you. This will allow you to light up all the possible positive changes and bring forgiveness to what you have to leave behind. Burn the letter to purify the energy surrounding it.

· 14. CRONE ·

Such mysteries I hold, but as one we build the story whole

14. CRONE

Compassion, deference, guidance

Such mysteries I hold, but as one we build the story whole

The earthly and the divine: there is a misconception of the incarnations being totally detached. However, the divine dwells below in every embodied being, breathing inspiration and creation into every moment of life. You don't have to pretend you are perfect, but you do have to seek the balance between what is embodied and what is not, between the extrovert and the introvert, between the moon and the sun and your yin and yang. Buddha in his enlightenment understood very well that to be you must find the right balance.

Understanding your creative role and using it on a daily basis makes you an incarnate angel; your responsibility as a messenger between the invisible and the visible is the work of your existence. If you are constantly watching, you can guide others to the entrance of their own path, so in a sense you are a priest, pastor or guide. Remain aware of the mission that falls to you. You are not a guru, because the one in front of you has the same powers as you; they just haven't realised yet that they're dormant. As the crone learned from her experience, wisely share your nature and knowledge so that enlightenment can spread.

Action: if others seek your advice give it with consideration. Be kind and try to understand what they are teaching you behind the exchange. Do not hesitate to support others, because that connects us all. Don't be scared to give, as you possess a lot.

15. SEED

Delays, patience, constancy

Grant me patience to hold still, as even when blind my vision is fulfilled

A seed is the perfect symbol of growth, representing both potential and its fulfilment because the cycle of life perpetually brings the fruit back to its pit, then to the tree and so on. As in nature, you do not escape cycles or their stages. Day after day you are the craftsperson of your own evolution, you learn and in turn you become a teacher to others. It is not a one-day job, hence the choice of the word 'growth', because you must first realise the potential within you in order to be able to harness, develop and enrich it until completion.

Visualise yourself as a seed, and if the results are delayed then remember that the roots are growing. Although on the surface nothing may be visible yet, in-depth wisdom extends more and more. Never lose hope and understand that you are life. This is exactly how your anamchara works with you: with perseverance and vision.

Action: work on your patience. List all the good things that brought you up to the point you're at to help you persevere in that direction. Read over the list every time you are starting to doubt and bathe in the feelings it brings. Keep hope like a lighthouse keeps watch. When things seem out of reach write to your future self, telling all you wish for them to have accomplished. Tell them how proud you are of them for their efforts and patience.

16. ENLIGHTENMENT

Bliss, understanding, communion

Night skies hide millions of stars; capture their light to lead you out of the darkness

There are moments when everything falls into place and just clicks as though it was obvious. Things unfold in front of you as the law of series, by which things happen more often than they should by pure chance. Embrace this moment, live it and celebrate it, and be at the heart of your emotion and this revelation. Know that those passages of life where grace touches you are not permanent but that you can come back to them, you can find them again.

When these moments arrive they are there to convince you that you are on the right track: it is a victory for you in the face of paralysing fear and blinding doubts. Allow this divine flow to invade your reality and mark in your memory the immediate impact it has on you, because one day or another you will be – perhaps even without knowing it – the instigator of this light for another being. Don't be afraid to lose this state. This is human; no one can live permanently in divine grace. Even saints have had their moments of darkness and doubts. Share the moments of grace through your self-expression to inspire others, in music, writing, painting or whatever form the message travels through to you.

Action: keep a memory of a state of bliss so you can get back to it again and again. It will become easier each time. Find a way to engrave the memory in your consciousness, such as a particular song or piece of music you can associate with the blissful state.

17. INITIATION

Teaching, repetition, obstacles

Bold and daring, I try again but differently to change reality

Have you ever observed days when everything seemed to repeat itself in a loop? If you're faced with repetitive patterns there is a lesson behind them. Indeed, the universe likes to repeat itself over and over again until you understand or take action. It is human nature to be very resistant to change, which makes it difficult to accept certain benevolent teachings. If you are not ready to accept and welcome the teachings then nothing will evolve.

When you are confronted by blockages you receive boosts from your anamchara, and although those boosts may not be welcome they are strongly necessary in order for you to move forward. Pay attention to situations and patterns, as there is a rite you must go through. Change your behaviour in the face of repetition so the outcome is different. Accepting and facing tests is always the fastest way to overcome them. Your primitive reactions are guided by ego and its need to survive. Fear feeds these certainties and locks you into patterns. You need to overcome this fear, because its projection is much more harmful than the consequences of its confrontation.

Action: the moment you realise things are repeating themselves your only choice is to change your attitude. Try to take a moment to think about why they are repeating and what lesson is behind them. Even if you do not accept it right away, acknowledging it is the first step to healing from destructive behaviour. Take responsibility and be a master of learning. If it has come to you, you can face it.

18. DEPTHS

Fears, introspection, inner strength

*Under your fear is the coat of strength;
to your song I answer in a prayer*

If you are experiencing an abyssal depth about which you have no clear measure, it symbolises both your fear and your unexplored potential. The incarnation that brings with it the fragilities of mortality has developed your anxieties of the unknown, of the unlived. You will wish to keep deep down this feeling that you are not exactly in your place, because your divine memory has been somewhat lost along the way. This sensation and millennia of painful incarnations undertaken mean you have forged an almost insurmountable wall between yourself and your deep nature.

Fortunately, that small divine voice within you is perpetually crying out tirelessly, until you are able to hear and trust it enough to act. It takes time and patience, but your anamchara never gives up and you will be left with a huge blank canvas and the opportunity to turn fear into perfect renewal. No matter how much effort it takes you do have to face this task, but you have all the tools you need to prevail. When you are ready you will pierce the stars of the dark sky.

Action: do some journalling to know yourself and understand what is blocking you or where and when a fear was born. Reflect on it, giving yourself the opportunity to accept your more vulnerable parts as they are also you. It is time to do some shadow work, to invite this vulnerability to come into light. Write your thoughts and experiences in a beautiful notebook that you treat with affection: it is a testimony of your evolution.

19. STAR

Joy, belonging, gifts

Blessed and blessing, may in you
my happiness spring

When you stop for a moment to gaze at the night sky where all those stars are shining, something simply and perfectly clicks into place: your smallness in this immensity, but also your role, your place in this natural and splendid universe. Give thanks that you have found your place, because you belong deeply to this world and your presence is as essential as any other. Celebrate this instance and fully delight in your joy.

Learn to receive as much as to give because this is how the embodied universe manifests: a constant exchange, a vibrating wave and energy in motion like the tides, lunar cycles and day and night. Placed in this whole, in your community, you bring your unique talent to this world. Trust that feeling and preserve it as long as you can. The Star card can represent a higher power, a person or an entity protecting you, as your immortal being knows what is good for your incarnation.

Action: you are protected and looked after, so take that certainty to materialise your dreams and give yourself to this world in becoming. If you have a project, use it as inspiration to express yourself. Now would be a good time to act, and even more if you also drew card 20. If you are fulfilled, enjoy every bit of it, give grace and welcome gifts.

20. TAKING OFF

Daring, making a move

Wind blows and water flows, pushing me toward my goal and giving me the lift to raise my soul

Don't procrastinate anymore! You have all the gifts you need, and now is the perfect time to stop thinking, get started and finally act. This card represents a moment of discovery, understanding and enterprise. No matter what area you are procrastinating on, today is the precise time to initiate the movement, to concretise. Discussions have no place, so put your wizardry in the gears of existence. You have sufficiently weighed the pros and cons, the possible and the impossible.

Overthinking and evaluating will generate a barren period when nothing happens, when nothing grows. If the grain is sown you must water it, so go for it and make your ideas a reality. Your action plan is exactly that: an action plan. Life incarnated is short, so seize opportunities when they arise. Don't be afraid to make mistakes on the way, as you have to experience all the possibilities brought alive by your dreams. Don't stay still just so you can avoid a wrong turn: take flight or a wrong turn, because it is sometimes unexpected change that gives life something bigger than you could ever dream of.

※

Action: your magical practice has no space here. This is probably the most materialistic card of this deck, inviting you into social actions and to expose yourself. Whatever drew it, its meaning is clear enough: move!

21. BALANCE

No duality, no extremes

No monster, no fairy;
my reality is drawn to equity

Existence is not made up of dualities or oppositions, but of a wide range of gradients you are too little aware of. Raised with the Manichaean archetype of good and evil, you sometimes forget that you come from a subtle mixture of eternity and mortality, hope and fear, power and submission.

When this card comes to you it would be good to reconsider balance in your life, between the divine and human terms, between pleasures and bareness. No one requires you to live a monastic existence, but to find fairness in your relationships with others and especially with yourself. Preserve the honesty and impartiality of a third party. Although it is easy to overindulge in any excess, your fulfilment lies in the osmosis between divine and human because that is what your present nature is.

※

Action: consider rituals to properly balance your
daily life. Discipline in practice can bring
a highly satisfying feeling, while unbalance shows
vulnerability underneath the excess that may
present itself as a virtue for an external eye.
Remember you are neither a sacrificed soul
nor a demonic spirit. Work on yourself via rituals
and meditation to balance what is disturbed.

22. KNIGHT

Honesty, bravery, detachment

I walk forth and across the mountains, keeping my north beyond all pain

A symbol of righteousness, the knight represents a sense of responsibility, of sacrifice. With the same purity, you are called to take responsibility for your life. If certain events occur unexpectedly it is totally up to you how you deal with the unforeseen and the unthinkable. A knight's honour shines through in critical moments when their actions remain kind and protective of those most in need.

This card calls you to detach yourself from the material world and act according to your heart, with love and generosity. Maybe you need to let go of what no longer serves you even if you are still emotionally attached to it. The anamchairde invite you to act to serve your higher being and not your ego, as through this sense of sacrifice you will learn to elevate yourself and serve your inner self better and more. Arm yourself with will: you are ready for this challenge.

Action: sacrifice comes with a sense of grief or loss and as a difficult choice to make, but if it is needed it is not necessarily bad. It is commonly said that beginnings are often disguised in ends, so try to see through, to visualise the bigger picture that goes beyond what you need to leave behind. Whether it is a habit, toxic person or job that makes you unhappy, the change serves the greater good, especially if the Knight card is drawn with card 18, Depths.

23. WOUNDS

Separation, grief, betrayal

I rest in you, spirit, so I can heal
and see through the storm

As unpleasant as this card appears to be, it presents itself benevolently to warn you of the danger in which you are advancing. It symbolises an event, an emotion or a situation that creates damage. Its nature can vary: a physical separation, a psychological tear, the loss of something or someone or even a betrayal.

You will have to detach yourself from your ego to overcome this state and learn the appropriate lessons.

Stop trying to act to please others and exhausting yourself in the process. Break the repetition of harmful patterns and get out of the mould that is suffocating you. Face the truth and accept the bad luck that has befallen you, because beyond this troublesome event lies a new situation that is healthier and free from any wounds. Even though you may not be fully aware of it, the current situation is working against you and there is a need to make way for a brighter future.

Action: make some purification and enlightenment rituals to give yourself some space for change. You could be so deeply involved in your situation that you may not even see it is hurting you really badly, but it is never too late and rituals are means by which to increase awareness of your patterns and habits so you can take back power over them. Try ablutions with incantations and burning sage.

24. MOUNTAIN

Being overwhelmed, hardships

No little step is too small, but many steps give a giant leap

Your current situation may be overwhelming you, especially if you lack the emotional distance to see it with a neutral eye. It is safe to stop, rest and overcome the hardships or accomplish the tasks one by one. There is a beautiful story about a woman speaking with her granddaughter on the way she overcame the horror of the Second World War when hope seemed to have no place. With wisdom and poetry the grandmother said that if it was impossible to consider even the mere next day then she just thought about taking things one by one: the laundry, a meal, pants to mend. She took one step after another like a re-education of life until she could project again, until finally a future became possible once more.

In the same way, do not be overwhelmed by the magnitude of things as one by one the breadcrumbs will guide you toward tomorrow. Your anamchara will accompany you.

※

Action: when a drowning feeling consumes you, breathe deeply and take baby steps. A self-love affirmation, saying 'No', cooking a meal or getting up in the morning: whatever you are facing, don't think about everything that is to come but solely your next step or what you can do. Each time you'll do a bit more until you can do a lot and until the mountain becomes a hill and disappears.

25. HERMIT

Being silent, stepping back, resting

In silence I retrieve; only if I ground first will I go forth

You are in need of taking a step back to deviate from the hustle and bustle of life and find your answers. Take the time to withdraw, to get down to meditating. Even if the moment seems inopportune or too busy, this card calls on you to silence all the useless and incessant noises of your existence to dedicate a moment to inner eternity. Your answers will present themselves to you if you allow time to work through the silence.

Your need for withdrawal is essential, so don't back down. You need to access your secret part, and in solitude comes light. In order to be able to re-evaluate your priorities and see life from a new perspective you have to go through a retreat. What I am talking about here is a journey to discover yourself so you can redefine your values, which will be a gateway to some wisdom and an open path to your anamchara.

Action: make a retreat in nature, go for a walk in the woods or by the sea or choose something that is close to you. It is urgent and imperative that you extract yourself from all the noise of your life. Reassess, breathe, let go: with new eyes you will be able to make the right choices. The Hermit card is always a call for rest and self-assessment.

26. FATE

Free will, karma, being masterful

Whisper, whisper, spirit of endeavour; may my heart be wiser and guide my decisions

Do you think that your existence belongs to you only if its course is predetermined? The truth is more subtle no matter how many lessons your soul has chosen to teach you through this lifetime and no matter what events seem undeniable. What matters is free will. You are not a victim of life; you have the power to constantly choose the direction of your path. You can live in anger, fear or love, and you can outlive any situation that seems insurmountable.

You are at a turning point, a key moment when you can live according to the codes determined for you or according to your own rules. There is neither limitation nor condemnation. Your path is unique to you, and you can make something extraordinary out of it every time. When you act, remember you carry your life. Each choice, whether to evolve or to destroy, will send back your own image. Karma doesn't forget.

Action: carefully weigh your choices then take responsibility for them. You are the protagonist of your life, its hero, so act accordingly and your book will be a masterpiece. It is your duty to remain the best version of yourself, and every night before you go to sleep you should take a moment to assess the choices you've made all day so tomorrow can start on the best foot.

27. THIEF

Hidden truth, manipulation, irresponsibility

Strange may feel the truth, but stranger will I be if I don't free myself

You may not be feeling worthy of what you have or find there are some truths that are too hard to face. Don't lie to yourself; this is not you. Be yourself, be truthful, push further and trust yourself. Forget the veil of illusions, as those characters you create for others are only masks. By dint of serving them daily you will end up believing they are your true face and get lost in them.

It's time to realign yourself, to take responsibility for your existence, actions and choices, but you must do this for yourself and not to meet any standard or dogma. You have moved away from the call of your anamchara, from your truth, and that is no longer enough for you. It's up to you to change things so you can return to a place where you feel comfortable. Lies and deception no longer have a place in your present. Take off the masks and make a clean sweep.

Action: you might like to present some apologies for your behaviour, to yourself as much as to somebody else. Lifting this from your shoulders will show you how you can get your own power back. When you direct your intentions to the right directions you are making yourself a gift.

28. CROSSROADS

Opportunities, choices, adaptability

Choice, choice, may not be; when there are too many I see what's best

You have opened the way to new horizons, but be careful not to disperse yourself too much. You are faced with the need to make a choice and are exposed to multiple possibilities. If the situation is to your advantage and places you in a position of strength, think carefully about the opportunities that arise in order to make a choice that suits you. Exploration and new horizons are yours. A great adventure opens before you, provided you know your plan of action well. Know the sacrifices you will be willing to make and the limits you will set, because knowing what you are getting yourself into is a great power.

You have the opportunity to grow wisely, extend your field of action and create to advance further if you learn to project your gaze toward your new horizon. Be creative to build your future but do not forget that it is your present actions that will build it.

Action: get outside in the sun and raise your palms toward the sky. Call upon the wisdom of the universe and let it guide you to make a choice that serves your higher self. Ground your bare feet on the earth and seek within yourself, because you already know how to act on the situation.

29. MASTERPIECE

Abundance, fulfilment, success

From air it starts, as thoughts, as dreams; beyond my own memory will it live to be

Rejoice, for you are accomplishing your work. In other words, you are on the right track and your efforts have finally paid off. This represents success and happiness but also the abundance achieved through your work; it is a manifestation of prosperity. The situation is developing and changing rapidly and blockages are breaking down, and your perseverance will be rewarded. If you are currently at a deadlock, don't lose sight of your goal because the result is imminent. As the wheel of fortune turns you come to the stage of accomplishments, when the reward is near and you will enjoy a sense of fulfilment from your victory. If it is right to enjoy this gain in your life then let it not be in vain. Winning does not make you better than others: you are simply at a different stage of your respective paths. Enjoy your happiness with humility and generosity but don't let your ego devour you.

This card also represents what you leave after you, the work you do not always realise you are doing but which will leave a light for others to pick up, just as the anamchara message passing through you.

Action: light a candle and count your graces. When fulfilment comes, think about turning to others to light their inner spark. The best thing about happiness is the ability to share it.

30. HOME

Hearth, love, comfort

When lost, I come to you; in flesh I am sacred, but in stone you are spirit

Everybody needs a nest, a shelter, a secret place where their soul immediately finds rest. This setting of love and peace nourishes and revitalises your soul so it can move forward. You are invited to connect with this essential place that protects you. Your body is your moving temple, but you also need a sacred space to connect with. Sometimes manifested by a person but more often a place, it is an invitation to focus on this source of happiness to draw all your strength in the face of daily life and possible events that may shake your foundations. It is time to pay a visit to your temple. A peaceful card, Home brings you a protective cocoon like invisible armour against the trials of life. If you do not have your own home, take the time and energy to create one in music, sensations and memories. It doesn't need to be physical: having it in your mind is like building a shelter.

While Hermit (card 25) indicates a need to retrieve from society and superficial noises, Home indicates a need to roost and rest. There is a sense of known energy in it that the Hermit card does not have, because the hermit is on a quest while you are at peace at home. The anamchairde are by your side.

Action: don't overlook the importance of roosting. You may go on great adventures, but what completes you are the tiny things along the way that create or remind you of a home. A sense rather than a clear representation, you need to nourish and enrich it as it will stay with you forever.

31. CONSTRUCTION

Rootedness, dedication, endurance

Time will tell how much I give, evolve and, piece by piece, how deep I build my kingdom

You have learned through many stages to deconstruct social and cultural patterns, transgenerational behaviours and bad habits that block you, but now you have to build. This is a moment of gestation, when you undertake a new journey toward your soul. You have an opportunity to build or rebuild the universal memory, to act on different bases, so act in a renewed way, fear not and ground yourself. If nothing is immutable and everything remains in motion, also know that if you do not follow this flow you will cease to 'live'. A new adventure awaits you; you must embrace it. The time is right for you to make a change, so hopefully face this new stage for yourself.

This card can also represent the necessity of holding on while going through a period of agitation. Don't give up when it becomes complicated or difficult, because you are able to go through. Stay strong like a lighthouse in a storm even if things look odd and unsteady. You have gone so far; you can do anything.

Action: stop hiding behind duties, schedules or anything that keeps you from taking action and trying new things. Your soul is craving fresh experiences, which is why you chose to be embodied. Ask yourself what you fear and whether that fear is worth conquering for amazing discoveries. Get out of your comfort zone, do something you have never done before and don't abandon this journey if you face a few trials.

Craftsman of dreams,
I see my own doing

32. PILGRIM

Humility, making amends, sacred struggle

Craftsman of dreams,
I see my own doing

You are and will remain human. Your imperfection sometimes tends to hurt yourself or others out of fear. When you draw the Pilgrim card it's time to right wrongs. Your anamchara kindly invites you to undertake the lengthy journey of the pilgrim who, recognising their faults and mistakes, chooses the path of forgiveness through their prolonged walk. It is an exercise of humility where the traveller, carrying very little on them, refocuses on their faith and advances with respect toward a place whose essential magic is reconnection with the divine.

You can be a pilgrim in your daily life by learning to see the divinity of the other, fighting for the planet and its inhabitants and holding them sacred. There are a thousand ways to be a pilgrim; it's up to you to choose your peaceful path. Light a torch and go forth, for the time has come to do something beyond your own life. It is the call of a life mission, like the grail quest. Maybe you'll choose to defend animals or shelter bees in order to save nature, but whatever your step is it matters.

Action: it might be uncomfortable to ask yourself if you were to die tomorrow what you would like to be remembered for or what your life would leave behind. Sometimes it is not so much about you but the light you inspire in others, who will go on to do bigger things. You are not ready to take on a war, but your love can move mountains. If it is not yours to move, may you light the way.

33. WITCH

Freedom, harmony, wholeness

Toil and boil, spirit of infinity; my seas of hope always spread wider

If you draw the Witch card your heart can sing. You have understood what serves your divine being, and have not only found your place but act in accordance with it. You are one with the world around you, aware of its constant miracles and filled with gratitude. The world belongs to you because you follow its flow with love. Just like a witch, you are a natural being who listens to their divine intuition and acts wisely. However, to live is to be in constant motion. It is complex to stay in this state forever and easy to be pushed down, so never lose this flame. Feed it and don't be afraid of having to go back down the ladder, because if you were able to reach this way of life you can come back to it without problem.

Don't let an outside cloud obscure the beauty of this clear sky. You have matured and can pick the fruit of life with grace. Whatever reward comes to you, you deserve it. It is not just due to blind luck but because you owned it.

❖

Action: write the song of your heart to remember later how strong you are, which may inspire others. You have wisdom, and it is now in your nature to share whatever you can to spread happiness. Enjoy, beautiful soul, every interaction, every spark. You had an incredible journey. It is not just a moment of light anymore; it is who you have become, and you can trust that if you went so far you can maintain that balance and beauty in your life.

34. FIRE

Playfulness, passion, intensity

Peace, tame my fire; and
playfulness, help me stay fair

The four element cards speak of balance and invite movement to fully live what is unfolding for you. They also warn against overflowing if you lose your balance. Fire, the element around which we gather and tell stories, is the element of admiration and joy. Who has never spent a long time lost in the crackling of flames? Fire urges you not to take things too seriously, to have fun whatever your situation, to take advantage and discover the joyful aspects of the task.

Be passionate, not allowing yourself to be devoured by duty or the importance of achievement. Life is the journey itself, and fire brings you comfort in the midst of a freezing night. Feel life feeding you this new energy and dance with it, but be careful as its intensity could blind you if you immerse yourself in it for too long. Learn to control your passion or anger through the joyful balance of fire.

Action: try to see your situation as a parody by undressing it from its dramatic aspect. It is not about throwing everything away but about lightening your spirit. Don't let anger or anxiety take over everything, as these are destructive feelings that will estrange you from your life. Put a smile back in your heart. A bad moment is never eternal unless you feed the fire with fire until it consumes you whole.

35. WATER

Flow, surrender, riptides

Torrents of life, in your wisdom
I bathe; spirit holds me tight

Water calls for fluidity in your life in order to destroy all the barriers you have erected. Indeed, these no longer have any meaning or raison d'être. The power of this flow of water and its density make it an emotional element. Beware of its depth, though, as you don't want to drown in it.

It's easy, especially when you're tired from a struggle that seems interminable to you, to let yourself be swallowed up by a hungry mouth, but remember that you shouldn't fight water as it will take you no matter what. Take a deep breath and just go with it. Make room for spiritual fulfilment so you can keep pace with the currents that sweep you away. It is in the long term that you will understand that this torrent took you to the magnificent sea of possibilities that will be offered to you. Stay hopeful.

Action: undertake rituals that include water, as they will help cleanse your mind and give you a fresh start. They also demand rigour in their practice, which brings balance to your thinking. Morning or evening ablutions are always a good idea as they prepare or repair whatever the day brings. Use your shower time to do some energy cleansing: as the water flows on your body let it free you from any undesired feeling that is pushing you in the wrong direction. It is an easy, efficient exercise that means each day can be lifted from its unwanted weight.

36. AIR

Open mind, being distant, dreaminess

I ground deeply but dance with
the winds; I live my reality

Air is an intangible element that requires a step back to see its effects. As it sweeps you up in its squalls it will give you a larger perspective, so look at the entire picture and don't get lost in the detail of the twirling leaves. See instead the tornado that shakes them. However, you shouldn't contemplate this display with too much detachment but should feel the wind in your hair and whistling coldly on your cheek. It will inspire you and seek to kindle your imagination thanks to the complementarity of all the objects it needs to manifest itself. Invisible but real, air will help you to keep your feet on the ground and your breath alive.

You are part of a movement that is shaking up your life. Don't look at it with an evasive eye, because this is happening to you for a specific reason. Stay in the dance, chase your dreams and use your wonderful mind to learn from your mistakes and perceive reality beyond mystery. See the world through anamchara eyes.

Action: ask someone close to you and able to have an objective observation of your situation to advise you. You don't want to be misinterpreted, nor do you want to get emotionally distant. You have the power to learn and evolve through your experiences.

37. EARTH

Prosperity, practicality, simplicity

Hands in soil, love is in the tangible as it is in the invisible; my treasure is abundance

Earth represents the physical manifestation of divine reality. This card won't tolerate nonsense and calls for practical solutions that require persistence and resilience but also simplicity, because if you know how to appreciate the value of this pragmatic work the reward will be beyond your expectations.

Use your senses to expand beyond what your eyes see. Underground, most of the work is done, and working the land doesn't require elaborate plans but rather love and patience. Don't get bogged down in complex ideas or strategies: approach things with simplicity!

Action: abandon your immediate plans and go for a walk in a forest or at the beach. Be a witness to the interconnectivity between plants, animals and elements, observing, admiring and finding gratitude in the smallest things. No schemes are required to get back to your situation. Set a new, clearer vision where you belong without having to elaborate in order to reach your goals. You don't need much to be deeply happy and are called to return to the essential.

38. SHADOW

Sacred feminine, shadow work, isolation

In darkness is born the moon, and beyond the night I rise as a new light

Contrary to what its name might suggest, the Shadow card is not to be feared. It is a peaceful card full of serenity that calls for listening to your spiritual being. It is the work of secrets, the inner journey to find your source. Light goes from inside out and is inspiration and creativity, the energy of yin, the sacred feminine and the immobility of a moment like an eternity.

It is the divine touch embodied. Be silent to receive the luminous messages but don't wander in this silence or wait for a response. Learn how to recognise the divine before your eyes.

This card of love, gestation and maturation is like a foetus in its envelope. It does not remain the same but is born and grows without measure. Leave some space for your spiritual growth, like gestation in the womb, but be careful not to let yourself drift away in this peace as the world awaits your light. Passivity is the warning behind this card as you can always see both aspects, good and bad, in every situation. Seek inner light within your shadows but don't sit there forever: rise again and seek your other half, the light.

Action: seek as an explorer, do some moon rituals and record your changes throughout its cycle. Consider calmness, silence, spirituality, feminine and divine energy, creativity, passivity and introspection, and when you get up in the morning ask the universe to help bring into the light what remains hidden and needs to be known.

39. LIGHT

Sacred masculine, manifestation, aggressiveness

Fire roots within and beams for others, as all negativity I banish

Magnificent is the light of the sun, streaming down upon creation and literally nourishing the world through the diffusion of its impalpable gold. Sometimes, though, it can burn and be too dazzling. This is the energy of yang, the masculine and the material. The extraordinary power that resides in embodiment invites itself into your life. Social beliefs and mass education tend to silence your power rather than nourish it, and make you blend in rather than giving thanks for your unique originality.

The sun must be celebrated. Of course, it's not about burning everything in its path to make things fit your vision, but there is a fine balance in respecting your successes. You are a being of talents, so manifest them and communicate your true nature, always with consideration and benevolence. As your light shines allow that of others to flourish, because it is your complementarity that makes your wealth.

Action: gain back your power, love yourself and go for it. Success comes to those who believe they deserve it. As the symbol of a stag, strength and royalty, you have to reveal yourself and your uniqueness. Do not do it by overpowering others but by inspiring them; they are part of you. When the sun comes down and you are alone, think about how others are playing a role in your bigger picture.

40. MIDNIGHT SUN

Boundaries, guidance, miracles

From dusk I guess dawn: I am the two faces that balance all energies

This card is probably one of the most positive ones to draw as it speaks of miracles, of improbability becoming reality. It evokes the spirit of the phoenix rising from its ashes and represents the power to say 'No', to set healthy boundaries in your relationships and establish something entirely new. You will no longer let yourself be vampirised: you have served as a slave for long enough and it is now the free child who expresses themself. You are a stronger being, a better version of you ready to offer yourself to the world. Your prayers have been heard and their answer manifests in your life.

You are at this moment in a sacred and protected place and guided by the purest love of the anamchairde. Perhaps you don't believe in yourself enough and this is addressed to you as an obvious answer. What you need will unfold under your feet naturally, so just look at this flower bed. Fly and do not try to hide your wounds because they have taught you how to become this new being. They are part of you, and as the phoenix is reborn from its ashes and not from nothing, let these be your wisdom. Welcome this truth and move forward serenely.

Action: take a moment during a new moon to reflect on all the challenges you have overcome and admire what you have achieved. Be proud of yourself and happy with the place you have reached. If life brings hardships, the person you are today is much stronger than the one you left behind so thank yourself for it.

41. YULE

Wisdom, generosity, honouring ancestors

*In the shadows we share;
all candles are bright*

At the darkest time in your life it is essential to remind yourself of your unconscious. We are meant to connect, share and feel as one, and from darkness rise the brightest of feelings, the very sense of existence. In the simplest gestures lie the purest nature. When you arrive at your bare minimum you drift away from futility and give sense and matter to every choice. At this barest you will show your true strength and will, because it is exactly there that your greatest wealth will be apparent in the impulse to get from your naked self to the abundance of the moment.

The winter solstice shows who you are, dropping all acts and recognising yourself in others. We are one, and your uniqueness completes us. Stay rooted and begin gathering, for tomorrow will shine from today's energy.

Action: at this special time of year make something for someone. Use your hands, time and intuition to connect with someone who has special meaning to you. Cook with love or build something: whatever your skill is, use it to show them they are essential. The true meaning of these celebration times is leaving out the superficial and connecting at a deeper level.

42. OSTARA

Health, priority reassessment, dispersion

Slow are my senses in the firework but steady is my race on the path of life

Life sprouts and spreads, an overflow that can be a bit intoxicating or at least distracting. Spring calls on your ability to observe, learn and grow. It is an amazing time of transformation and perturbation whether it is in the weather or in the display of the earth element. If you sit still and take time to contemplate all the work that goes into the change, baby step after baby step, nothing becomes so natural and obvious than this explosion of possibilities.

As spring blows on everything with its wings widely spread, you are called to become a communicator. Understand, give, pass on: you are like a busy bee pollinating or the wind carrying seeds further away. You are a piece of that tremendous equation and have a role to take on.

Action: grow a plant from scratch and put your intention into it, and all the love and energy given to nurturing the seed will grow into manifestation. Believe in your own power and the incredible strength of your desires, then take pictures or make sketches of its evolution and put some more visualisation into it. You'll discover the amazing results this brings.

43. LITHA

Rewards, saving, spending

Harvest as attention goes to the little things; today's care is tomorrow's offering

While everyone enjoys the light in the exuberance of summer months, there is a secret language behind it. Welcome the shadow that comes next. Do not use all your strength at once, as you will need it further down the path. If you celebrate the longest day of the year at the summer solstice you may tend to forget you also welcome the decrease of light, and the fact that important work needs to take place gathering every little thing that will take you through the colder months. Make jams and candles and pile up magical herbs for your health and beauty potions.

When you are at your best you need to count your graces and fill your stockings. A conscious gratitude when you are facing prosperity means you can welcome less straightforward times. Keep this thankful spirit of plenitude flowing. Behind the apparent recklessness of summer lies long-term work for your children, your future generation: what do you want to leave them with? Everything you create today will keep blooming tomorrow, but if you neglect or overlook the duties of transmission you'll be left with very little.

※

Action: every day presents itself as a blessing. Honour what is given and may be taken away by drawing a circle with salt, sand, earth or any symbolic form. Bring inside it during a full moon cycle all the graces you want to say thank you for, with trinkets representing those. When the new moon presents itself you may do the same work, but let go of things that do not serve you anymore.

∞ ※ ∞

44. MABON

Awakening, mustering energy, magical powers

Guide me through, as at the gate
I am with your power at hand

Just like spring, autumn is a doorway. Spring opens onto life and autumn onto death, shadows and mystical worlds. It is the portal for magic. Reaching its peak at Samhuinn, when the departed are celebrated, this season is called the season of the witch because of all its magical occurrences. As earth takes over in an explosion of colours just before the quiet silence of winter months, you are invited to dive more deeply into your spiritual capacities. You should question yourself and call upon the invisible to guide you through the shadow realm of winter.

Autumn is a teacher for the inner self while spring is for the outer self. When you have experienced the wheel of seasons and reach the blazing one, all the marvels within you need to now come out. Know yourself fully; trust yourself fully. Follow the witchy path, picking nuts, berries, laurel and more. Construct a broom to sweep your front door and keep your inner light on.

Action: this is the season of the witch, the season of magic, when you should cultivate your abilities for the invisible. Give yourself time to explore divination art, meditation and spiritual growth by communicating with your anamchara. It does not matter if you lead a busy life, because if you don't make time for this in autumn you never will. Autumn is an open doorway to the spiritual world.

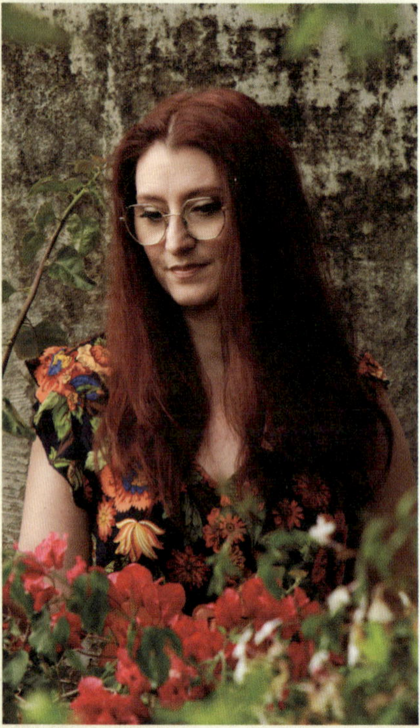

ABOUT THE AUTHOR AND ILLUSTRATOR

Born into a family of artists, Saorsa Sionnach was a contemplative and discreet child who connected intuitively with the natural and subtle worlds. She found in the craft the freedom of exploring and honouring all the sacred aspects of life and recognises herself as an elemental witch. Her roots and travels shaped her spiritual journey, but it is her Scottish descent that truly set her on her life's path.

Saorsa currently lives in the Canary Islands, the primal energy of which led her to define how she could turn the messages she channels into a tool for people to reveal their own powerful potential. She believes we all are limitless and gifted the same way. Beings are meant to be connected and have one great consciousness with many expressions. The right path is our own, at all times.

Optimistic and free spirited, Saorsa distils her knowledge and sense of wonder into colourful illustrations and incantations for happiness and light seekers.

@saorsa.oracles